From This Good Ground

Effie:

I enjoyed this,
and hope you
will, too!

Love,
Bert

1974

Edna Hong

DESIGN AND DRAWINGS BY KAREN FOGET

AUGSBURG PUBLISHING HOUSE

MINNEAPOLIS, MINNESOTA

From This Good Ground

To my father, Otto Hatlestad
to my mother, Ida
and to my brothers and sisters
Agnes
Carl
Margaret
Alfred
Joseph
Eleanor
Bernard

Contents

I love my fate to the very core and rind. . . . I was born in the most favorite spot on earth, and just in the nick of time, too.

HENRY DAVID THOREAU

I regret that I have no gloomy and savage father to offer to the public gaze as the true cause of all my tragic heritage. No pale-faced and partially possessed mother whose suicidal instincts have cursed me. . . . I cannot do my duty as a true modern by cursing everybody who made me whatever I am . . . I am pretty sure that most of it is my own fault.

G. K. CHESTERTON

Preface

"*The trouble with you, Mom,*" *said one of the five* sons one day, "is that you never really left Taylor County, Wisconsin."

"Thank you," I said at the time, quietly pretending to accept judgment as compliment, which is about the only way to disarm a male offspring when he begins shooting at his mother's halo. "I suppose you are right. I suppose I never really did leave Taylor County, Wisconsin."

"But," I added, many months and many musings later, "why should I? If the good God gave me such good ground, why should I leave it? The good ground of a good childhood—the most precious resource on this planet!"

"The joy of being a child I have never had," wrote Søren Kierkegaard, tortured on the rack of chronic mental depression and guilt, both real and imagined. "The frightful torments I experienced disturbed the peacefulness which must belong to being a child . . . for my inner unrest had the effect that I was always outside myself."

Unlike Søren Kierkegaard, I had a happy childhood. Is that why I have almost always been *inside* myself? Is that why I have never felt the need to revolt, have never needed to "escape," never needed to "live my own life"?

Not that I cannot and do not espouse Causes! I marched with my husband and two youngest sons in the anti-Vietnam war protest marches and caught the murderous glares of the Veterans of Foreign Wars on the curb and heard one of them remark contemptuously, "The dirty yellow cowards have even got their mammas along!"

Indeed, I even seem to have acquired somehow and somewhere the aura of a Liberated Woman! At least, students pushing the college administration for the pill once invited me to speak on their behalf, but I spoke instead on behalf of chastity and invited them to join me in the clandestine Underground Chastity Movement to which I belong.

So never really leaving Taylor County, Wisconsin, does not necessarily mean that the Wisconsin-child-self merely became an old and older and still older self. It means that a happy childhood in Wisconsin somehow helped one self to become all the more a self.

Consequently *From This Good Ground* is not an attempt to tell the unimportant story of my life, but rather to explore how a happy childhood helps one to be genuinely what he or she is. Nor was it written to ride the current nostalgia wave, but to reveal how a native nostalgia for God was not rendered comatose in the backwoods of Taylor County, Wisconsin in the twenties.

There is a why as well as a how behind this backward journey.

"The trouble with your generation," said a student not long ago, flicking a crumb of my homemade, homeground wheat bread from his Jeremiah beard, "is that you have taken everything real and natural out of food, fun, instincts, environment—out of everything — and our generation is simply trying to put it back."

"Yes," I said, cutting him another slice of bread and spreading it thick with wild raspberry preserves, "and you and your generation make a religion out of putting wheat germ back into the bread and sex into your fun and saving the planet to save your own skins."

"And for whom else should it be saved?" sputtered my Jeremiah friend.

"Maybe for *heaven's* sake," said I.

"What do you mean?"

"I'm not quite sure! But I have a glint of a meaning, and frankly it floors me, for it may mean that you, my anti-establishment friend, are an instrument in God's amazing supernatural grace. Yes, you! You and your army in patched bib overalls! Can it be that the Supreme Salvager himself is using you to salvage us human beings? If so, I am ready to be as amazed as I am amused. And to be grateful!"

Perhaps it all ties up—"never leaving Taylor County, Wisconsin" and salvaging us humans as well as planet earth!

Anyway, *From This Good Ground* is a timid tentative attempt to tie a knot by someone who never even won a Girl Scout badge for tying knots.

The Parental Soil   1

If a computer were to be asked if the natural ground my parents provided for the natural growth and development of the self of their sixth-born was good ground, it without a doubt would add up the facts and deliver an emphatic *No!* And to emphasize its answer even more it would, computer-fashion, print it a 1000 times.

In fact, were the computer to be asked if my parents should ever have been married at all, it would probably spit out a quick answer amounting to: *Grossly incompatible! All wrong for each other! Marriage doomed to failure or to producing a disruptive home.*

To put it as tersely and bluntly as possible—two

people with very disparate natures fell romantically in love, married without any financial security or professional counselling, and without being "ready for parenthood" in any way but physically, haphazardly produced eight children, of which I was the sixth.

Moreover, Child No. 6 arrived unwanted and unplanned in the bleak midwinter in the bleakest period of their lives, when the arrival of yet another child was an embarrassing inconvenience bordering on disaster. There was no cow in the cowshed, no hen in the henhouse. As a matter of fact, there was no cowshed or henhouse. There was not a silver dollar in the pouch father kept under the mattress. Moreover, my parents were strangers and newcomers to northern Wisconsin, far from the Valley of Relatives in southern Minnesota, far too from the community of Norwegian Lutheran friends in Madison, Wisconsin, where my father had worked as a machinist until the doctor told him to go to the farm or die an early death.

Reflecting its desolate-by-every-standard start, the child that blundered into this world the cold end of January, 1913, did not gain one ounce for the first three months, not until the cow father bought with his first earnings cutting timber "freshened" and mother was able to supplement the thin blue milk from her undernourished breasts with a porridge made from flour and milk from the cow's bursting udder. *Grøt,* the family called it, for they still spoke Norwegian in the home, although the children going to school in this "Yankee" settlement were beginning to answer the parents in English. *Grøt* saved my life. *Grøt* stopped three months of wailing and made it possible for me to laugh into the ruddy and kind face of Pastor Midtlien when he baptized this child of total strangers who suddenly appeared one Sunday morning at his church in Stanley, Wisconsin, driving in from the "backwoods" in a borrowed buggy with a borrowed team, and disappeared before he could fill out the baptismal certificate or learn the address. My sponsors were recruited from a newly confirmed class in the congregation—all strangers to these total strangers!

And *this* botched-up beginning was good ground? *This* was assisting and enabling and encouraging to the development and growth of a healthy, well-adjusted human psyche? What could this mis-matched marriage, this accidental birth, this un-promising, impoverished milieu provide but child-hood traumas? Surely, surely, by all the laws of men-tal ill-health, this parental soil was hatching ground and nursery of animosities, regressions, repressions, obsessions!

Grøt may have saved my physical life, but my psyche was saved by my being born early in the 20th century, before its later-born women were quoted in the national news media as saying, "Who wants all that garbage with babies and husbands and junk like that?" Before marriage partners were led to be-lieve that living with one sex partner 'til death do us part was hell on earth. Before the vexations and frustrations of marriage and having children were violently stirred up from the bottom, where they

21

naturally settle when they are accepted as the normal sediment of life.

My arrival at that particular point in time certainly was dismaying to my parents, but they did not recoil from this unplanned fruit of their pleasure in each other and curse the "accident" that produced me. They accepted me with the same sturdy trust in life and in God that parents in those days accepted "another child." For them January, 1913, was the worst possible time to have "another child," but they *naturally* wanted children, it was *natural* to have children, and they accepted another child into the family *naturally*. I added nothing whatsoever to their security, ease, and comfort — in fact my constant starved wailing in that too small, too hastily erected, flimsy house must surely have subtracted considerable security, ease, and comfort of mind from the world that was my family. However and nevertheless, it was a *natural* world into which I entered, and I had a natural place in it.

As for the disparate natures of my parents, it can be summed up simply by saying that I whistled and sang in father's presence, never in mother's. For her "whistling girls and crowing hens always came to some bad end." Also, "If you sing before breakfast, you will cry before supper." Mother was Law. Father was Grace. Naturally we children preferred to be in father's presence. Rooting around in my ancient tendencies, I begin to suspect that I very likely became a tomboy and a girl of the outdoors to escape the discipline and duty that reigned indoors. It was more fun to milk cows and cock hay in the relaxed presence of father than to mop the kitchen floor and iron shirts under mother's critical scrutiny.

Does this mean that father was permissive and loveable and mother was tyrannical and hateful? Mother nagged and bitched and father slank around like a whipped dog? Mother wielded the rod and father spoiled the children? We children adored father and despised mother?

Not so! Not so!

This was the pre-Ann Landers era, and the weekly columns in the local paper and farm journals discussed the mating problems of cows and bulls, pigs and boars, and the problems that arose in rearing *their* offspring. Incompatibility was an existential fact, but it was not—at least for my parents—an ugly marriage-mangling, home-destroying fact. Ida Nordby and Otto Hatlestad simply wedded their incompatibilities as well as their compatibilities in a relationship that anticipated no threats or dangers and defied the world, the devil, and Old Father Time.

Conjugal love it is called. Theirs was a Christian conjugal love, for they had made a sacred and solemn vow to the Christian God before Pastor O. A. Bu in Bloomfield Church, Ostrander, Minnesota, and were sincerely convinced that their marriage thereby was armed against any foe. My parents had a lot of common sense but little psychological knowledge. The God of my parents, however, was not so super*natural* that he did not understand or was not concerned about the precariousness of the natural irresistible and powerful affinity between Ida Nordby and Otto

23

Hatlestad. He saw the opposites in their natures when they themselves were love-blind to them. He was not an enemy of their erotic attraction and romantic love. As a matter of fact, he was so much a friend that he placed this natural love of theirs in bond, guaranteeing that this love shall be preserved in marriage.

It was preposterous even to think that the conflict between father's easy-going nature and mother's devotion to duty and strict regime would or could ruin the marriage, so neither father or mother gave it a thought. One does not fear what is not anticipated. They accepted each other's opposites without trying to amend them, although there of course was some psychological breaking-in on both sides. Father, who had grown up in a relatively unregimented family, learned to appreciate the comforts of a systematic life. Perhaps there was not much excitement in knowing that on Monday he got oatmeal for breakfast (and without sugar, sugar was bad for the teeth, and never mind if he was all that used to it from home); on Tuesday, hot graham muffins (Mother called them gems); on Wednesday, corn bread; on Thursday, buckwheat pancakes, etc. etc. One learned to be grateful to have a wife who got out of bed in the morning and served her husband such a breakfast. Perhaps father's pipe-smoking and tobacco chewing scandalized mother, for whom any self-indulgence was a sin, but she let him keep this sin if he promised not to visit the bootleggers (during prohibition) or stop at the corner tavern (after prohibition).

So, without shaking the foundation of the marriage, without father being emasculated or mother oppressed, the opposites were worked into a common ground. Detritus soil it could be called, for it was the loose material resulting from the natural breaking up of rocks. By an elemental process the rocks of conflicting natures in my parents' marriage crumbled into a loose soil permeous to the flowering of grace. Held together by a solemn vow to God and to each other, it was their incompatibilities that broke up and not their union. Had they allowed their incompatibilities to break their union, their powerful natural attraction to each other would never have become a cherishing love, a preserved and preserving love—that is, conjugal love.

Mother, the Mineral in My Soil

Now when I look back across the chasm of mother's death, I realize that love is not one element, soft and gentle and persuasive, and duty another, hard and stern and repelling. Love tempers duty. Duty tempers love. There is no conflict between law and love when the law is love and love has the "thou shalt" of the law. The unity of the two makes for well-tempered and tillable ground where the self can deeply and firmly root. At least, so it was for me.

My reliable memories date from the move to the Taylor County farm the spring after I turned seven, and the mother I remember from that period in my life lavished duty on me. But I am not being sentimental or trying to be charitable when I declare that she must have lavished love on me in those infant years which psychologists insist predestine the tendencies. In my most malleable moments I must have been rocked and stroked and fondled and called pet names in Norwegian in the very same way I saw mother make darlings of Eleanor and Bernard, the two who followed me. In fact, the very same way she petted all of nature's helpless babies—all the kittens, puppies, chicks, lambs, and calves that were born on the farm. One of my pre-Taylor County memories (proving its indelibility) is of mother weeping for hours in her bedroom because our puppy had blundered onto the road and had been run over and killed.

The reason I am sure that I basked in love when it was very important that I do so is rooted in another memory—that every time I became ill in the night (childhood illnesses have a habit of striking then), I groped my way through the dark hallway and down the stairs to mother. Not to father, for he obligingly departed for the couch or the bed I had just vacated, provided it was not defiled by vomit. I crept into father's warm nest beside mother, and it was mother who cradled my misery, stroked my head, and murmured over and over again a word that echoes in my memory as *Stakkars! Stakkars!* The Norwegian dictionary spells the word as *Stakkels*, but whatever the spelling or pronunciation, I knew what it meant: "Poor little thing! Poor dear!" The word was loaded with all the love and sympathy my stricken self needed. It did not matter that the hand that stroked my face was workworn and that my hair caught and pulled in the cracks.

But the minute the cute, cuddly animal babies and the animal in her darling human babies needed to be trained, mother became law and order. Wasting no time in "channelling aggressions into more constructive activities," she channelled her children onto the straight and narrow path of obedience, order, work, and responsibility. Just as the gangly puppy who piddled on the kitchen floor had his nose thrust into the puddle and was cuffed out the door, the human cubs who tracked mud across her freshly mopped floor were verbally clouted and made to wipe away the footprints. Mother's weanlings were not very long out of the crib before they learned that "No" did not mean "Maybe," to disobey was folly, and if order was not heaven's first law it certainly was hers! To throw the well-regulated machine of her daily routine out of gear by any arbitrary act of self-will on the part of her children was sedition, and there was no appeal beyond the supreme court of mother. We read mercy in father's eyes, but his lips never spoke the countermanding words. Did he perhaps accept mother's role as trainer and disciplinarian in the family because he recognized that what she had to give was the nutriment his own life needed—and ours, too?

Not that we did not sometimes chafe and burn at this trimming and pruning of the constituents within our human nature that are less than divine! "No" is a hackle-raising word at any age, at any time. Humankind has no rind so dull and impervious that it does not prickle with resentment at denial and restraint. We children did not assume the burden of being civilized by mother without some furious frustrated tears or private tantrums. The long low sheepshed roof was a splendid place to lie on one's stomach and gouge one's eyes with clenched fists while the feet hammered the shingles. Even as an adolescent I found the sheepshed roof a refuge from mother's adamant "No" and a palliatative for my rages. Singly and in pairs we children sometimes ran away from home, but never beyond sight of the roof of the big friendly red barn and never so long that we were missed or that we missed a meal.

Just when and how and why mother's law turned into grace for me and her *no* became a *yes* within me, I am not sure. My sudden realization that this mystery had taken place in me came long after I myself was mother to eight. It was a particularly busy day, "with all my irons on the fire," as mother used to say, but I paused to read a letter from my sister Margaret. "You can depend on it," she wrote half seriously, half ironically, after a long account of her awesome activities. "Any man married to a Hatlestad girl is a pretty lucky man!"

"Why, of course!" I exclaimed aloud—and ran to read the unadulterated, undisguised truth to my own lucky male.

Under the rigorous training of mother we four girls, whose human natures certainly cannot be said to have taken to tasks as a duck to water, have learned to work. We accept the ordinary responsibilities of life with a natural and utterly un-self-conscious cheerfulness. Our happiness does not strand on menial tasks. All those repetitive household tasks that could have diminished or demolished us are *second* nature to us and hardly demand our attention. In fact they scarcely interfere with whatever cerebral work happens to be going on in the upper storeys. Indeed, they even seem to facilitate creative contemplation!

Thanks to mother, who regularized and normalized and systematized (in my vocabulary these are not dirty words) the machine in us, we daughters can prepare "a threshing-crew dinner," bake bread and apple pie, set an attractive table, wash and hang out clothes—all at the same time and all quite swiftly and effortlessly—and all the time capable of carrying on a lively conversation with anyone present—or with ourselves, for in all this we remain present to ourselves.

At worst mother's motivation for all this training and discipline may have been to present the image of a "nice family" to an admiring community. At its best, her motivation may have been obedience to her Lord, who told her to "train up a child in the way he should go." I will never know her unvarnished motives, but her results are as transparent to me now as the windows had to be when we helped her with the spring housecleaning. Our big family of father, mother, four sons, and four daughters was not permitted to be at the mercy of the sins of its individual members. We did not realize it at the time, of course, but mother's law protected the family from the unblunted hurts and harms of each other's human nature. Mother was no theologian, but she was no sentimental optimist about children either, and she did not mistake childish innocence for human perfection.

Were mother to be hauled before a tribunal of Liberated Women she would promptly be judged and condemned to outer darkness for raising up four daughters who are Nest-Makers (there is nothing more contemptible in the realm of Militant Ms's). But mother would dismiss the trial—as she would dismiss the whole movement—by calling it "a peck of foolishness." And if the Liberated Women would take time to scrutinize my mother and their own mothers with anything but a baleful, jaundiced, prejudiced eye, they might be surprised to see that they did not suffer from negative self-images, they did not feel victimized by male chauvinist pigs, and did not hate the double bed. Nor had they bartered their need for protection for the need for sex. They did not continually and frantically ask themselves, Am I failing my husband? Is he failing me? Am I failing my children? Nor were they supermothers with a madonna syndrome, creating mother-haters of their sons and menopause-neurotics of themselves. Nor were they sweet little, dull little homemakers, neutral beings like Samuel Johnson's country gentlewoman, Lady Bustle, "whose great business of life is to watch the skillet on the fire, see it simmer with the due degree of heat, and to snatch it off at the moment of propition, and the employments to which she has bred her daughters are to turn rose leaves in the shade, to pick out the seeds of currants with a quill, to gather fruit without bruising it, and to extract bean-flower water for the skin."

No, mother was no Lady Bustle. Nor was she the sort of woman Peguy declared would "tidy God himself away if she came to heaven one day." As a matter of fact, there was a blessed lot of freedom in all of mother's law and order. She was by no means a compulsive or fanatic housekeeper. The bedroom she shared with father was no starched, ruffled and chastely feminine showpiece which father hardly dared enter until he slid between the sheets (there are bedrooms where it is difficult to imagine the man in the house even daring to do that). Father took his afternoon nap there and put his feet on the bedspread. As for the children's rooms, they were truly our own rooms if we made our beds daily and hung up our clothes in the closet and chased the dust kittens from under the bed once a week on Thursday. Having earned the right to "own" our room we could possess it freely. We cut paper-doll families out of last year's catalogs and populated our rooms with them. We arranged and re-arranged the furniture to play school, church, house. Or we shut the door of our room and remained alone with a book. For that habit, too, the habit of reading, we got from mother, for she insisted on "peace and quiet" in the evening so that she could assimilate every printed word in *The Lutheran Herald, The Prairie Farmer, The Wisconsin Agriculturist, The Taylor County Star-News*—and always and always her favorite devotional book, *Streams in the Desert*. After darkness fell, there were but two alternatives for us children in a country home without electricity—to join the readers around the hissing Coleman lamp—or go to bed. No wonder we became

33

readers who read every morsel of print we could lay our hands on, be it good, bad, or indifferent.

If mother had been unable to relax into her own world of mind and spirit, I suspect that we children would have been damaged by her too earnest concern on our account. However, if she was reasonably sure that our alimentary canals were functioning healthily and healthy habits were being grooved into whatever part of the anatomy of the brain that habits groove, and that our inner being was forming a healthy core, she could and would neglect us. We throve in that healthy neglect.

In the same way, we throve on all the tutelary laws, although at the time we did not know it. What child does? Why do we seem to need the distance of death to see the straight and narrow path as the road to freedom and the enlargement of the self? That is, if the straight and narrow path is under the sun of love and love is sovereign—as it was for us. Of this we had final proof in mother's dying. After a stroke at 82 and three days in a deep coma, she came back for one brief lucid day. Incredibly, all the "ought" and "must" and "thou shalt" and "thou shalt not" was rinsed out of her, leaving the radiance of love that had always been there like the red in the maple leaf which emerges only when the leaf is dying. The flame was there all the time. Her sometimes roguish self danced in her limpid blue eyes, and her face was wreathed in smiles. She stretched out her arms to her children, and we went to them—not like slaves of her law—but like children of the love that was sovereign in her.

Eleanor and I teased her that day. "You know," I said, "someone who knew you when you were young told me that you were very beautiful. She said that you were the belle of the county. You had four daughters, mother, but none of your daughters comes up to you in beauty."

"Oh, ptt!" she exclaimed. "You're talking a peck of foolishness!"

Father, My Humus 3

"*Will you teach me how to milk?*" I asked him one
summer evening as I teetered on a three-legged milk
stool behind the cow he was milking, sometimes
watching the rhythmic squeezing of his strong hands,
mostly watching three kittens lapping up their supper
of warm foamy milk at my feet.

"How old are you?"

"Nine going on ten."

"Well-l, maybe you better just milk the cats," he
said, chuckling.

"I'll learn just as good as the boys! Really and truly
I will!"

So I started to practice on Grandma, a gentle old
Jersey cow, who turned her head questioningly and

rolled her great Greek eyes and breathed her grassy breath on me, but went back to her cud-chewing and allowed me to tug and pull and squeeze her teats without protesting. It took a week for my weak-wristed attempts to transform an unconvincing spurt to a steady singing stream of milk into the pail. When father began calling me at 6 A.M. when he called the boys, I knew that I was finally "worth my salt" in the barn and no longer "not worth a straw." The brothers, of course, were happy to give me first two—then as I grew more competent and could even fill a pail as fast as they—three and four cows. But father would not let them assign me the just-freshened milking heifers, who protested this bizarre handling by clubbing with their tails and kicking with their hind feet, sometimes stepping in the pail.

Why did I, unasked and unforced, cheerfully exchange delectable mornings in bed for getting up in winter darkness, pulling on overalls and jacket stiff, cold, and redolent of cow, to stumble from the house, the domain of my sex, to the barn, the dominion of men? Why did I, as yet an unfettered child, spontaneously offer myself as a slave to a milch cow? For bondage it certainly was and is. Farmers may think themselves the masters and the cattle their fenced-in chattel, but whether or not the human masters are up-and-coming or pottering or puttering, *they* are the fenced in ones, bound by a stern practical—indeed, a moral—responsibility to feed and shelter, board and room, these cows—to say nothing of a stern responsibility to relieve the cows of the burden of their milk.

My psychic structure is as deformed and difficult as any "normal" human being, but I have rooted in vain for any sordid unmentionables to explain my voluntarily choosing the work which placed me in the company of my father. It was simply a matter of the heart responding to the initiative of grace, of walking toward the light. Merely by being what he was, father practically condemned me to doing what I felt would please him. It was, if you please, a matter of the pleased self desiring to please what pleased it.

There is no doubt about it—father was pleasant company. He had a way of being present to us that helped our fledgling selves say, "I am." His eyes did not ignore his children or rest on them and say, "You do not amount to anything *yet*. Maybe someday— but right now you are less than nothing."

Yes, there were and are farmer fathers with a practical, utilitarian attitude to their children much like the attitude describd by Thomas Kyd in the sixteenth century:

> . . . And what's a son? a thing begot
> Within a pair of minutes—thereabout:,
> A lump bred up in darkness, and doth serve
> To ballast these light creatures we call women;
> And, at nine months' end creeps forth to light.
> What is there yet in a son,
> To make a father dote, rave, or run mad?
> Being born, it pouts, cries, and breeds teeth.
> What is there yet in a son? He must be fed
> Be taught to go, and speak. Aye, or yet
> Why might not a man love a calf as well?

Or melt in passion o'er a frisking kid,
As for a son? Methinks, a young bacon,
Or a fine little smooth horse colt,
Should move a man as doth a son;
For one of these, in very little time,
Will grow to some good use . . .

And I—I was not even a son!

My favorite time with father was helping him with the chores on winter Sunday afternoons when the older brothers were having their kind of Sunday afternoon fun in the neighborhood, and the big sisters congregated somewhere, too, and spent their time singing "Barney Google with the goo-goo-googly eyes" and "Yes, we have no bananas," all fifty-some verses. Father's usual gentle slow pace and good humor were better or best on Sunday afternoon. While he tended the bull and the horses, I measured silage to each cow and topped each mound with a gallon-pail of feed. To the cattle the feed must have been equivalent to fudge frosting or strawberry jam on toast, for they shook their stanchions impatiently, waiting for me to come with it. As I drew closer with their dessert, they got down on their knees, stretched their necks, extended their thick tongues, rolled their eyes and tongues obscenely, and snuffed and snorted with unseemly greed. Quiet and contentment reigned only when we had made the rounds and every animal was crunching and munching her Sunday supper.

The colder the weather outside, the thicker was the frost on the spikeheads and boltheads on the inside of the big barn door. The colder the weather outside, the more of a haven was the barn. Once the stock was fed, the barn exuded an animal contentment and security that communicated itself to all my country senses. There was the sweet-sour smell of cud, which is simply fodder regurgitated and chewed in quiet rumination and animal contemplation. The sound of the cud-chewing produced a thrumming and a humming that made it seem as if the barn itself were purring. The mist of moistured air meeting cold air pushing in from the cold windows enveloped me as I knelt in the clean straw and tickled the new batch of kittens into a frenzy of playfulness. Chores finished, we hurried from barn heaven to kitchen haven where the teakettle sang on the Home Comfort range.

The wood-burning cookstove is associated with another grateful memory of father. No matter how fully and carefully stoked with popple chunks at bedtime, both the kitchen stove and the furnace in the cellar went out in the night. The first one out of bed in the morning was always father, and before he called the milkers, he rebuilt the furnace fire, shook down the ashes in the kitchen range, laid a bed of chips and spindling kindling, and started the fire. When I came down, barely awake and shivering, I found him hitched up to the stove, his feet propped up in the open door, smoking his morning pipe. I pulled the kitchen stool up to the stove and scrunched beside him, feet in the oven, hands buried in the sleeves of my old sweater. We said nothing. The snapping and crackling of the fire said it all, assuring us that the chill at the marrow bone of life would pass and civilization would survive. Or was it father who without speaking communicated that message by some sort of spiritual osmosis? After ten minutes or so of this ritual of "seizing the day," we put our toast-warm feet into our shoes and went out into the winter cold.

The boys clung to bed-warmth longer. They arrived in the barn seconds later than we, but without the ritual, without their bio-psychic equilibrium secured for the day.

There seem to be two classes of men: one cannot or refuses to accept the horror in life, the other accepts life complete with all its horror. Both classes have their great exponents. Father did not know the exponents, but the fact that he did not ask questions of life—or ask them aloud—seems to indicate that he belonged to the latter class. If he had remorse about the past, guilt about the present, or anxiety about the future, he did not betray it to his family. Even the constant threat of losing the farm to the Federal Land Bank—a farm he bought at high boom time and did in fact lose in the depression—did not engulf him in black despair. At least he did not inflict his fears on us, and we grew up feeling very comfortable and secure in the universe.

It could be argued that both father and mother should have shared their disquiets and insecurities with us, that we should not have been allowed to grow up certain and secure in so uncertain and insecure an age. And so ignorant of the injustices of man to man and the wretched misery of most of our human brothers and sisters. But that dark enlightenment came soon enough! It does—inevitably. By the time it came to me, I had grown a core of confidence that did not shatter under the impact of all that dismaying knowledge. Was it because as a child I could say with Thoreau, "I have heard no bad news"? May not the constant exposure of children to dismal and despairing "news" dry up the juices of the heart and grow a rind of callousness?

In all honesty it must be admitted that we children did know about the existence of that mortgage, for I distinctly remember looking for clams on the muddy shores of the creek that lounged through our land and praying fervently before opening each one that there might be a pearl of priceless worth within which would pay off the mortgage. This romantic hope derived from having read a sentimental novel which I believe was called *The Blue Moon*. The author himself had gone from farm to farm selling his own book— and the impossible dream. The Horatio Alger books also fed my dream, for in them the rags-to-riches hero suddenly appeared at the foreclosure sale just as the auctioneer's gavel was falling for the third stroke. But there was no "Blue Moon" pearl in the clams. Father lost the farm he bought for twenty thousand dollars in 1920—a debt he managed to reduce to ten thousand when the depression hit. The farm was hardly worth the ten thousand he had scraped together over the years.

Mother had never wanted father to buy the Taylor County Farm. To her it was moving to the "backwoods," for the farm was twelve miles from the nearest high school. Apparently she made father promise that every one of us would get a high-school education —a promise that he faithfully kept. And patiently!

His patience must have been severely tested and tried in the winter months when he had to bring us on Sunday afternoon to Medford by sled, for the country roads were not plowed of snow in the twenties. Moreover, it was the "old plugs," the solid stolid work horses, who pulled the sled. To keep us warm on the long journey he built a small shelter on the sled (we called it a house-sled) and put a small wood-burning stove inside. Winter after winter he fetched us home on Friday and back to our rented room ($4.00 a month with kitchen privileges) in Medford on Sunday. Patiently and with never a grumbling word.

Nor did father grumble in the month of May at the high cost of educating his youngsters. It was in May that the frost came out of the ground and the township roads took on the appearance of battle grounds. It was not just a matter of ruts getting deeper and deeper and the ground becoming softer, until even the high-slung cars of the twenties rested on a sea of mud while the wheels spun impotently. No, May after May certain sections of road seemed to become arenas for tortured internal convulsions that heaved and humped the surface and finally cracked it open to spill out mud as shiny and slippery as axle grease. "Frost boils" they were called, but the name does not adequately describe the wreck and ruin of road, especially after futile attempts to travel or bypass them. Farmers unfortunate enough to live near such mudholes kept their teams in harness ready to rescue the foolish with a chain and whiffletree.

Father could have left us in town during the worst of the bad roads, but he did not. He knew that his children were farmer class, and farm kids in those days did not commingle with city kids. He knew that a weekend in town would be a long, long loneliness. So—though the roads be hub-deep in mud, somehow father always got us home, even if it meant miles of detour to avoid the utterly impassable seas of mud.

Certainly we must have gotten stuck once in every mud season, but I cannot recall it. Perhaps if father had blown his tension in a rage that cut a wide indiscriminate swath and assailed everyone and everything, us children, too—then perhaps I would remember those times. But father stowed his tensions in a silent, secret corner of his mind—which perhaps explains why he sometimes took to his bed for a day with what undoubtedly was a migraine but we all knew as a "sick headache."

The atmosphere he created around his children was as free of violence and fear as it was of censure and threat. He did not scold or berate any more than he exhorted or admonished. Tease he did so, but there was no pain in his teasing. It merely told us that he delighted in our company and thought we were jolly good fun to have around. He wrestled with his sons even after a fringe of gray hair crowned his bald head and he detected that his six-foot sons were letting him pin them. He goodhumoredly played the double-indulgent game of indulging father to the very end, which came unexpectedly and in great agony on the night of August 5, 1939, after a heart attack among the haycocks on a torrid, humid day.

My partner and I, wed but a year, were camping that night on a mountain in Norway, and no ESP notified me of my father's death. But of one thing I am sure: being loved by my father as I was and loving him as I did created the crucial precondition for loving the man I married, the male who shares his life with me and I with him. If father had been a tyrannizing father, practicing either the tyranny of cold inattention or aggressive attention, had he been a competitive "keep women in their place" male chauvinist, I, too, perhaps would be up in arms against all males.

Grateful for Eight!   4

Sometimes when our children seem to concur with advocates of abortion on demand and agree with them that the fetus is not human and has no right to live, we remind them that if our parents had held the same view perhaps neither we nor they would exist, for their father was the fourth baby and I the sixth in our respective families. "And if we had stopped at two, six of *you* would have been aborted. Which six should we have denied life?"

As for my own family constellation, which neither I nor my parents chose but accepted as one accepts the rhythm of the seasons, I cannot conceive of my life without any one of them. Collectively and individually, they helped set me in the mainstream of existence. They helped educate and equip me to live in today's world, which certainly is not a comfortable place for the fainthearted and fearful. Without them I would not be as flexible, adaptable, and unsinkable as I like to think that I am.

For I do not believe with 17th century John Earle that a child is "the best copy of Adam before he tasted of Eve, or the apple." An Augustinian in theology, I believe that a human infant enters life bearing the image of God, but also seeded with sin. "It is the physical weakness of a baby that make it seem 'innocent,' not the quality of its inner life," said Augustine.

Nor can I, reared with seven brothers and sisters, believe in the myth of the old-fashioned rural family, "God's little country," living in perfect peace and harmony. Nor do we, having reared eight of our own, have any illusions about being a model Christian family—no more than we have any illusion about having been reared in a model Christian family. God be praised, there was and is no prototype Christian family. Any "such a nice Christian family" can only be a caricature of a true Christian family, and caricatures are not to be copied.

We squabbled plenty, we eight Hatlestad children. We were all born with organic tissue that reacted to irritants, and we reacted, bristled, ruffled, and provoked in the natural human way. We lived in the same environment, but each of us had received a different set of genes from our parents, and our personalities collided. But children's quarrels do not last long when parents do not interfere, and our parents did not interfere. Not because of indifference or neglect, if you please, but because rural parents are too busy to be everlasting child-watchers. Nor need they be, for generally speaking the farm is a near-perfect playground for spontaneous, unsupervised play. When we played King of the Hill on the rotting straw stack, no parent was present to reprove if the incumbent king instituted a reign of terror. We kids imposed our own discipline in our own way, out of sight and sound of parents, and the dethroned king thereafter humbly played by the rules. When we converted the granary into a schoolroom and I, playing the teacher, insisted on tenure (long before tenure was written into teacher contracts) and refused to be demoted to pupil, my pupils simply absconded, and I was left with an empty schoolroom.

It was as simple as that! The perverse little ego inside each one of us that demands to be the center of everything was snubbed and cuffed and knocked into some semblance of civilization. We did it to each other. We mended, amended, and emended one another. If we were soft on anyone, it was to the "baby of the family," and he perhaps is the first to admit that this may account in part for his sometimes being soft on himself. The Old Adam in us certainly was not annihilated—that takes divine effort—but he had his rough edges trimmed and blunted. In short, we learned to live in community with other human beings.

Our subsequent emigration into the larger human family did not come as a rude shock, for we were not greenhorn emigrants in a foreign land. We knew and know what a confounded compound man is, for by living with each other we learned to know ourselves, and by learning to know ourselves we learned to live with others—and with ourselves.

We loved as fiercely as we squabbled, and just as squabbling whipped us into humans that could live with other humans, loving each other educated us to find our way to loving other humans. Someone has said that the use of loving one person is to be educated in finding one's way to all the rest.

Again and again we died the frequent little deaths that close-knit families experience when loved ones are absent—the absence proving beyond a doubt the quality of the presence! We moped around in a miasma of blues when Agnes, our oldest sister, left home at seventeen to go to North Dakota, where she could teach without a normal-school certificate. We wept unashamedly with mother when her favorite son left the farm to "go out in the world and make a living."

My memory of Margaret leaving to attend St. Olaf College (which she "worked her way through") is tinged with self-irony, for I realize now that I distinctly enjoyed the experience of wading in the Slough of Despond. The Model-T Ford with father taking her to the Soo Line train in Owen passed the one-room rural school just at opening exercises time (9:00-9:15). It happened to be the morning teacher played records, and we could choose. I asked for Stephen Foster's "Old Black Joe." "Gone are the days when my heart was young and gay," wept the baritone, just as the Ford bearing Margaret away for an eternity of time went by the window. I placed my geography book between the other children and my tears and dampened two handkerchiefs—but relishing each tear. Certainly the emotion was not phony; but it was the first, and by no means the last, time I fondled my pain.

All of which reminds me that I could so easily have isolated myself in moods and daydreams, for nature had dealt me a strong propensity for both. I dread to think of what I would have become had not these self-isolating inclinations been rudely refused me by my siblings. If I went to the attic to daydream about the handsome new seminary student who was "filling the pulpit" in our rural church (could he, would he fall in love with me, a mere farm girl, and wait for me?), my brothers and sisters inevitably invaded the attic and converted it into a play-church and made me pretend *with them* instead of all by myself alone. Not to be jerked from my romantic dream, I demanded to be my secret beloved, the seminary student.

"No, you take up the collection."

"But I don't want to take up the collection. I want to be Mr. Odden!"

"Then you can't play!"

Thus, out of sight and sound of parents, we eight children were saved from an inadequate view of the complexity of human nature and learned to cope with each other's complexities—and perhaps to some extent to control our own.

Being the sixth child gave me the enrichment of both older and younger children in the family. In fact, the oldest of the older children in a family often complete whatever incompleteness the parents may have. If a mother is short on mirth, the oldest sister may be long on that ingredient. If a father is not keen on sports, an older brother may be a crackerjack in all of them. If parents are shy about sex education, the older sisters and brother can explain its mysteries to the younger ones.

Agnes was my second mother who patiently did for us younger kids everything mother was too busy to do. In fact, I preferred to have her braid my hair, for mother did it so tightly that the braid pulled the scalp. Mother's washing our heads was a no-nonsense performance that all were relieved to have over and done with. With Agnes it was a game where we sculptured our sudsy hair into a towering headdress and postured before the mirror. "Mirror, mirror, on the wall! Who is the most beautiful of all?" "Snow White!" said Agnes, pretending to be the mirror—and the Witch Queen ripped down her coiffure and pranced in a rage around the room, shaking soap foam into the air.

Carl, Alfred, and Joseph, my three older brothers, are as different as they can be, proving that corn, cabbages, and cucumbers all grow in the same ground. I loved them and trusted them, and together with father they were my door to the world of males and the principal reason I did not slam the door to other males or all males in general. But open to each other and intimate with each other we were not, for proximity without intimacy was as sadly true of me and my brothers as it is of most families. Hence my astonishment in World War II to discover the name Joseph

Hatlestad near our own on a list of Lutheran pacifists. Without reading Tolstoi, Gandhi, Thoreau, or any of the current peace literature, Joseph had come to the same difficult decision my partner and I had made. And I, who had been with Joseph many times after pacifism as an alternative to war had exploded in my sky like a cosmic comet, had never discussed it with him. What trivialities had we talked about—the weather, the price of eggs, the crop outlook?

"I guess we were too close to each other to see each other," I said ruefully to my partner. "Joseph and I were too familiar with each other to see each other deeply or to find anything astonishing in each other. I suspect that close-upness in family living is tantamount to closed-upness, not closeness."

The enrichment of younger children in a family was provided by Eleanor and Bernard. Being displaced as the baby and hence the coddled favorite of the family is supposed to be traumatic to a child, but I must have become a displaced person willingly, for I can find no scars. Did I know that it was absurd to try to compete with this cute blonde roly-poly baby that laughed her way into everyone's hearts? But a competitive child feels a sense of defeat if he is the loser, and I felt nothing but sheer admiration to see my toddler sister make any and all company bright and lively with her saucy impudence. Her wit and her tongue have never lost the tartness it received from the sauce of tender teasing by her family.

To come downstairs one March morning and discover a new baby brother might seem sufficient motivation for asking some curious questions: Where did he come from? Why is mother in bed? But I remember no curiosity whatsoever. Indeed, I was two years past womanhood, all of thirteen years, before I learned where from and why and how babies came. The new baby brother was pure gift, and one does not ask where gifts come from or how much they cost. One merely hangs adoringly over the crib and worships this new creation, every tiny crinkled finger and toe of him.

Bernard made Eleanor and me a trio, and my childhood memories are always of "the three of us." Because there were five older than ourselves we perhaps were allowed to run unleashed longer than the others. With no media to divert us, no organized recreation programs, no Blue Birds, Girl Scouts, or Boy Scouts to entertain us, we created our own entertainment and diversions. Faced with all those hours of "nothing to do" we were forced to encounter our own moods and surmount them. Were we impoverished and disadvantaged kids? Reflecting on our past plight in these days when kids are barraged with entertainment, enrichment, and improvement programs, are toted to and fetched from a variety of self-improvement lessons, are instigated, motivated, and activated into proper activities, turned, twisted, and bent in proper directions—I am sure that the poverty of programming in which we lived was more stimulating to our imaginations than the present wealth of schemes to energize creativity in children. Perhaps the deprived child is not the child with no toys and no projects but the child with a nursery full of toys and a week crammed with planned goals and targets.

What did we three do with all that "nothing-to-do" time? One summer we "canned" feverishly, collecting all the discarded bottles and jars we could find and filling them with all the flower and weed "fruit" we could pluck. After cramming the jar full of "fruit" we filled it with water, capped it tightly, and placed it in the row of "canned stuff" in the capacious sled-box sitting in the sun behind the granary. Strange mysterious forces went to work and created horrendous brews which certainly would have exploded had we not uncapped them every day to sniff and exclaim in wonder and revulsion. Our stock of preserves accumulated and the vintage improved— that is, emanated ever more grotesque odors. I am sure now that we had quarts of camomile tea, which Peter Rabbit had to drink as a medicated punishment and which Europeans still drink for every ailment known to man. I am also quite certain that we preserved marijuana as well as other "dangerous, habit-forming drugs." But we did not drink or eat our fruit, nor did we inhale it for mind-blowing experiences. Just what was fulfilled in us by this diversion I do not know, but the game did not pall for days, nor did the odors.

Come to think of it, far from living in a wasteland of options, we three, growing up poor on a farm in Taylor County, had a gold mine of options. We could play tag in the swamp, leaping from squishy hummock to squishy hummock, shouting with laughter when one of us slipped off into the murky muck and had to pull his feet out with a mud-sucking sound. We could choose to be engineers for the day and dam the creek, gathering stones from the fields and, staggering under their weight, carrying them to the scene of our project. No doubt we toiled harder and sweat more than any slave or stevedore or hired man, but it was toil without moil and sweat without tears, for we were our own masters. By the end of the day we had not created the lake of our dreams, not even a pond, but without knowing it we had raised the level of that quite private sea in our subconscious, that sea of memory that years later can brim and spill over into the consciousness at the slightest stimulus. So sensitive is the valve to this subconscious sea that a whiff can trigger it.

With the irrationality of kids we sometimes engaged in one of our most strenuous sports on the dullest and hottest July day—flushing woodchucks out of their holes. Our interest in woodchucks was already aroused by the silly rhyme:

> How much wood would a woodchuck chuck
> If a woodchuck could chuck wood.
> A woodchuck would chuck as much wood as
>   he could,
> If a woodchuck could chuck wood.

If one of us discovered a woodchuck excavation in the pasture while fetching the cows, we went back together to search out his alternate escape hatch. The next day we pumped all the pails we could find full of water and lugged them under the broiling sun to the scene of our strange sport—sometimes two or three city blocks away. With one of us standing guard at the second hole, the other two sloshed the water into the first hole as fast as we could. Suspense and excitement! Was woodchuck down in there or not? Would he come out or not? Would our investment of time and sweat and muscle pay off or not? Sometimes we lost the gamble. Woodchuck was not at home or had moved to another apartment. But sometimes the scout posted at the other hole let out a shout and we rushed over just as woodchuck emerged from his back door. Was our sport savage? Hardly, for we did not club him, we did not stone him, we merely laughed at his drenched befuddlement. Was it silly? Perhaps—but remember, it was July and 90 degrees in the shade, and sometimes the only antidote for that is silliness! And it cannot be denied that the sports we three invented proved the dynamics of boredom!

Tasks we did have, but those tasks we could do as a threesome were more game than work. One of the happiest of such tasks was carrying lunch to the haymakers, for it meant picnicking every mid-morning and mid-afternoon. Thick slices of homemade bread generously spread with homemade butter and slapped together with a crisp lettuce leaf sprinkled with sugar. A jug of freshly pumped water (that abomination, Kool-aid, had not yet been invented). Huge crisp man-size white sugar cookies or soft moist molasses cookies spiced with ginger. All this eaten on a haycock throne under the benign June sun in the relaxed company of father and big brothers, who never appreciated us more than then.

One of our self-created pastimes during the making of the hay ended in tragedy and points up the

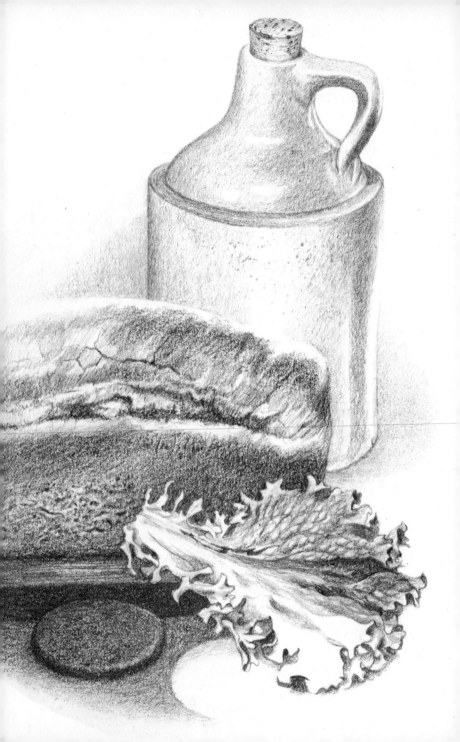

responsibility thrust upon me as the oldest member of the threesome. Maude, an old and retired horse, was left at the barn to pull the hayfork with its clutch of hay up to a pulley track where it slid back into the dark cavern of the hayloft and was dumped into the haymow. All the skittishness had drained out of faithful old Maude and she was judged safe enough for us kids to lead and to ride up and down the slope to the haybarn. We were not warned against the horse but against following behind the whiffletree lest something break and the whiffletree be catapulted back and kill us. There was always a true-life story to back up these admonitions.

But no one thought to warn us of what eventually happened, for our own capricious imaginations were not to be anticipated. While father and the boys were in the field, we three decided to lead Maude, hitched to the hay fork rope, up and down the slope. We took turns leading the horse, the other two standing at the top of the slope behind the pulley through which the rope snaked. While I was leading Maude, Bernard, suddenly dissatisfied with the limp and laggard way the rope was rising to the pulley, grabbed the rope and braced his four-year old body against the pull. A knot slithered up and pulled his left and foremost hand into the pulley. Maude and I heard his scream and stopped. I turned and saw the frayed and mangled flesh that never again shaped a tolerable hand.

Our treble screams brought father and the boys across the field with the hay wagon lurching and the work horses at full gallop. It brought mother running from the kitchen, her face contorted with fear. But it was another contortion that sent me to hide in the farthest and darkest corner of the empty sheepshed.

"Now see what you have done!" she cried, her face dark with anger, as she and father drove off to the hospital twelve miles away with Bernard still screaming between them, his mutilated hand swathed in clean towels.

I did not question the accusation, I did not dodge the guilt. After all, mother was right. I was the oldest, I should have known better. Lying face down on the musty straw of the sheepshed, I cried and keened and assumed the whole load of guilt. Desperate suicidal plans marched through my mind, but fortunately I eventually fell asleep and could not attempt them. In a stupor of despair I slept hours, and it was hours before they found me. Fortunately, too, it was mother, my chief accuser, who found me, and her relief when the inert form of her sixth child stirred under her groping, searching hand was such that she burst into tears.

"*Stakkars! Stakkars!* You couldn't help it! I didn't mean what I said!"

And I awoke to weep afresh, but this time mother's tears mingled with mine, and the miraculous power of forgiving love began its healing. I was accepted back into the family, and no one ever blamed me again for the deformed hand. Not even Bernard. By the grace of forgiveness, the adhesive that held our decemvirate and triumvirate together did not yield, proving again that love is tougher than iron, stronger than steel.

The Church in   5
My Disputed Ground

The Diamond Jubilee booklet of Our Saviour's Lu-
theran Church, Holway Township, Wisconsin, pictures the church council of the jubilee year, 1963. Of
the ten members pictured three are my brothers:
Carl, Alfred, and Joseph.

"Quite natural!" my anti-Establishment, church-
dropout friends would say if I imparted this informa-
tion to them, "Your parents probably believed that
being good church members is synonymous with being
good Christians. They very likely instilled your brothers' unwary understandings with all their religious
clichés, pious reflexes, and cargo of Christian dogma,
and your brothers are not intellectually sophisticated
enough to get rid of all that tripe."

To that I would perhaps snap, "My brothers and sisters and I happen to prefer all our religious clichés and pious reflexes and Christian orthodoxy to pop psychology, mushy mysticism, and all that tripe. We happen to prefer the symbol of the Cross to that of a rebellious seagull. We happen to believe that we are not OK and neither are you!"

"You talk like a fundamentalist!" they would exclaim.

"And what's wrong with fundamentals?" I would say.

Whereupon I would borrow heavily from Reinhold Niebuhr's *Leaves from the Notebook of a Tamed Cynic* and ask them if they, who are so fearful of corrupting their children's minds with "superstitions about God," were teaching their children the English language and thus robbing them of the possibility of choosing German, French, or Japanese as their alternative language. Were they withholding Bach and Beethoven from their children in order that they might be free to prefer Stravinsky?

Says Niebuhr: "Nature has wisely ordained that faith shall have an early advantage in the life of the child to compensate for its later difficulties. If we imagine that we help the progress of the race by inoculating children with a premature sophistication, we are of all men most miserable."

It is perfectly true that Carl, Alfred, and Joseph very likely would not have been on the church council if father and mother had not been church-goers and church-workers and had not resisted all the forces of hell, high water, and hard winter and brought their children to church every Sunday. It is quite true that I was already inoculated, indoctrinated, and dogmatized by the age of three when I toddled before the congregation the night of the Christmas program and shrilly proclaimed:

> I'm just a little girl.
> I'm only three years old.
> But I wish you all
> A very merry Christmas!

I mean that at the tender age of three I had already fallen in love with the church, and I have never fallen out of love with it. Pathetic preachers, shockingly incompetent Sunday school teachers, bad interpreters of good doctrine, fanatic fundamentalists and fanatic disgruntalists—none has disaffected me in my love affair with the church. Somehow grace seemed always to be able to press in on my small soul in spite of myself and those humans who with the best of intentions plug all the ingresses of the soul.

I do not deny that soul-pluggers are present in the church, sometimes in the guise of Authority, Trained Experts, Celebrity Preachers. I do not say that memorizing the catechism letter-perfect, reciting the books of the Bible the fastest, learning the dimensions of the ark and the precise route of Paul's journeys did anything but make me conceited about being the prime pupil in the class. Teaching methods in the Sunday schools of my childhood were deplorable. They still are—when teachers forget that religious knowledge is to be communicated by contagion, not taught, and that the communication of religious knowledge ought not ape secular teaching.

What I am trying to say is that in spite of imperfect communicators, a dearth of teaching materials, and no visual aids whatsoever, something was communicated to me by the church in my home and the church in my community. Because of that communicated something I am not sleep-walking in the desert. Before a dull, impervious rind could grow over my soul, my life was set in perspective to time and eternity, to the temporal and the eternal. Before longing, man's umbilical cord to the eternal, could dry up and dissolve from disuse (although I do not really believe this is totally possible), the numinous-arousable me was set in relationship to him who planted the numinous and arousable in me.

Oh, God did not shout his presence to me. Instead of experiencing him as the Hound of Heaven, as did Francis Thompson, I experienced him more as Philip Toynbee does, more in the "guise of a very shy rabbit, constantly disappearing down his hole." What the church in my home and the church in my community did was to develop a potential planted in me into a condition of mind and spirit that acknowledges the presence of God. Not as a superlativity but as a positively present. An ever-present hope in him. Someone has said that every child comes into the world with the message that God does not yet despair of man. The church in my home and the church in my community did not extinguish that hope but built upon it, so much so that never in my darkest moments has my hope in him flickered. In fact, it burns brightest when my hope in me is darkest.

Just now as I write this my favorite FM station is playing Vivaldi's "Gloria." Outside my window my favorite maple tree is playing The Burning Bush. And the tears stream down my face! For these ecstatic tears, for this unutterable joy, I thank the church of my childhood, which never, never played Vivaldi to me and perhaps still does not know his music. But it carried a live coal from the Burning Bush to my spirit; it communicated to me the glory that the "Gloria" sings.

My mother's deadly home devotions did this to me? Those endless boring hours in the summer-hot or winter-chilled white-frame church of my childhood did this to me? That absurdly foolish recitation of meaninglessly memorized catechism did this to me? Is not the whole church Establishment and System supposed to be the chief quencher of spirit in a child?

That it is not so is the mystery of the church! Although much that is done in the name of the church almost smothers the uncertain fire that burns in its members, although many of its planned programs create more smoke than fire, the church *nevertheless* cherishes and proclaims the word of the living God. And the word of the living God can and does break through with urgency even through poor and unworthy proclaimers, stale systems, and lubberly establishments. The crucial point is that the word is planted, the word is there—to break through!

The word of God has been coming to me through

more or less imperfect instruments all my born days, and I thank my church for those humble servants who stammered and stuttered that word to me. I see them not as quenchers but as keepers of the flame. Keepers of the flame sometimes are wrongfully accused of being quenchers, but their gift is not to add kindling to the fire but to keep alive what has been kindled. Curse them not because they did not blaze, but thank them for keeping the weak, guttering flames in themselves and in us alive! Bless them for being the bearers of the word, imperfect though they were.

For children, at least for this child, the word of God received from the church in the home and the church in the community was like a time capsule that activates in the spirit at some future date. Not a pink pill for a pallid spirit now, but an encapsulated encounter for some engulfing moment in some then, in the fullness of time. Even now, half a century later, the capsulated word of God explodes in my mind and spirit, and a verse that shed no light for me or on me the first time I heard it—or the tenth—or twentieth time!—suddenly illuminates. At such times I understand how the Sleeping Princess must have felt when the prince kissed her and woke her from her hundred years' sleep!

The Holway Lutheran Church was three and one-half miles from home, and when the roads were blocked with snow father put the wagon box on the sled, covered the floor thickly with straw, and lined the box with blankets. Here we usually sat snugly and warmly while the team plodded through the drifts to church. But not always—for sometimes the cold was so bitter that it invaded straw and blankets and crept into our blood and bones. The climate of the uninsulated frame church did not reverse the polar trend. The preacher in his high pulpit above the heat register was the only one present who was warm. Trotting behind the sled on the return journey restored our circulation, but the chill lingered in the marrow of our bones for hours after we reached the warmth of home.

Surely bringing a big family to church in the winter in the 1920s was no easy matter (or in any season or decade for that matter). It did not just involve getting us all to church and back. Sunday actually began on Saturday with the polishing of all the shoes. A second pair of shoes "for dress-up" we did not have, but the plain old everyday shoes were brushed and blackened and rubbed until they shone like new. To make Sunday the queen of the week the girls and mother baked cake and pies on Saturday. Before we left for church Sunday morning, the potatoes were boiled, mashed, and ready in a double boiler on the back of the kitchen range. A pot roast was left in the oven to stew in its tender juices until we came home. More often than not the minister and his family came home for dinner, especially in the months of benign weather. After the benediction, mother watched the other women with a sharp eye, and if no one else invited the minister's family, she did.

On the three festival offering days father led the procession around the altar, and I am sure no one left a larger bill than he on the altar for the pastor. Even

71

though he was losing the farm he did not diminish his support for the church and the minister. And how many dozen eggs and chunks of fresh butchered meat and ears of sweet corn did he and mother, along with other good farmer souls, stow away in the minister's car before he came out of the church with his black valise?

Why did they do it? Why did they bother? Why were they not simply satisfied to be nice people, good citizens, decent neighbors? Why did they drag the church into their lives, into their children's lives?

Unlike what, when, and where questions, why questions march through the accidentals and incidentals of life, through the second nature to the unplumbed depths of the first nature. By making the church so important in their lives, my parents forced me later in life to ask why?—and searching the answer has been one of the most fruitful searches in my life.

In the homemakers' columns of the *Wisconsin Agriculturist* and *The Prairie Farmer,* mother read the current nutrition news and promptly translated it into her own kitchen. Long before organic food was a fad, she was most concerned that what went into us was natural and wholesome and that what came out of us came naturally and regularly. Indeed, I am surprised that we Hatlestads are not permanently tinged a faint green for all the lettuce and greens she fed us. But without ever studying theology, anthropology, or any of the other -ologies, mother knew that a child is more than an alimentary canal with an ingress and an egress.

Father was as deeply concerned in his role of provider for the family as mother in hers as dietician, and we eight never went shoeless or coatless. But he did not have the world's obsession for more and more shoes and coats, a closet stuffed with shoes and coats, a bank stuffed with money to buy more shoes and coats. He knew that there were other ends to life than that.

By having us baptized and naturalized (enemies of the church say "habituated") into the church, mother and father placed us into a world we could not at the time realize and into a community of love for which we were not ready. But we were *there*. We were not foreigners, outsiders, strangers to this world and this community. Without our willing it so, we were moved into this world and this community when we were weak and defenseless, and this world and this community have been moving in on us ever since.

So I thank my parents for not placing me painfully outside the church but *inside*, where the Word could get at me—sometimes painfully—and bring me to the center and source of gaiety, Jesus Christ.

I thank my church for placing the idea of *ought* into me. True, the *ought* and the *nots* were taught me first, and true, they sometimes were shallow and superficial *ought nots*. I was first taught that it was bad to steal, swear, and have a baby out of wedlock. But under the tutelage of the Word and the Spirit, the *ought* manifested itself until I could see that often the very goodness of the "good people," myself included, was selfish self-interest and disobedience to God's ought. In short, I learned guilt.

If there are those who think it is far preferable to

be pagans without a sense of guilt, let them only look about the world at the "happy pagans." Let them scrutinize the modern world without an *ought*, this world of the conditioned and the conditioners who have no norm, who believe there is nothing *true* or *right*, who talk about what is right for the whale but will only admit into discussion what is *useful* for man. Yet to quote again that exposer of charlatanry, G. K. Chesterton:

> We speak of a manly man but not a whaley whale. If you want to dissuade a man from drinking his tenth whiskey, you would slap him on the back and say "Be a man." No one who wished to dissuade a crocodile from eating his tenth explorer would slap it on the back and say, "Be a crocodile." For we have no notion of a perfect crocodile; no allegory of a whale expelled from his whaley Eden.

Let those who think it is preferable to be pagan look at this total descent into an oughtless world without a sense of guilt and see its desolation not as an accident but as a symptom.

I thank my church not only for inculcating me with the idea of ought, but also for giving me a concept of healthy guilt and a conviction that there is no place for vanity in me. For guilt, because guilt is the only way I have to know when I have hurt someone I love. For a conviction that there is no place for vanity in me, because it keeps me from fleeing to self-improvement programs. The only flight possible for such as I is to Jesus Christ. There and there only I learn to hate my faults and failings without resentment and despair. There and there only my spirit receives from Holy Spirit the power to break the oldest rhythm in the world, the rhythm Henderson in Saul Bellow's *Henderson the Rain King* calls the worst suffering known to man, the repetition of a person's bad self.

One of my favorite childhood songs was "The Bear Went over the Mountain." What the bear found on the other side of the mountain was only the other side of the mountain. The church took me over the mountain of my sin and there I found the Kingdom of Grace. And every single moment of every single day is transformed—not that I enjoy the here and now *as it is,* enjoy the world *as it is.* This is another modern idea that teeters on the edge of heresy. Here again the word which my church cherishes and brings to me reveals that it is not the transient present world as it is that I am to enjoy—but Christ in its concreteness, the perpetual power of his love at work in the world here and now.

Disputed ground I was and am and will ever be in every hour of my life in this world. This truth my church has taught me, and it is one of the dark truths that blesses when one does not flee from it but swings around and confronts it face to face. But the church also teaches me that I am not a helpless, hopeless comic trapped in an absurd existential situation—as modern literature would have me believe. The church sets me in the community of the undismayed and undaunted who cling to Jesus Christ. And Jesus Christ, please note, *clung to the tradition of the church,* but purified it with his life and death and renewed it with his purifying Spirit.

When all is said and done, this is perhaps why I am most deeply grateful to the living institution of the church and will hang with it: it is the only institution I know which has the principle of and the power for ever-recurrent renewal.

Sweet Grapes
of Wonder

6

Taylor County is not famed for its natural beauty,
and, as far as I know, no poet has exalted it in verse.
Its northern boundary is the doorsill to the wooded
lake country, and its southern boundary is the fag-
end of good farming country. "Marginal land," I
think it was called in our geography book, and we
understood that to mean that Mother Nature had
more or less disinherited our county. At least her
small farms had to be wrested from scrub popple,
underbrush, and the litter of stones abandoned by
tired glaciers, and after all that the soil was not by
any means rich Iowa loam. Moreover, there was no
romance for us Taylor County natives in stone hedge-

rows, for they were symbols to us of hours of stoop-labor behind team and stoneboat.

However, children do not demand the ineffable and the unutterable in nature, do not ask for a setting of grandiose dimensions and extraordinary beauty. We learned this from our own children when we brought them to see the most spectacular wonders of the West. At Crater Lake the children were entranced with the tourist-tamed chipmunks. At the Canyon the chief attraction for the children was the train of tiny burrows climbing up the narrow trail from the canyon floor with their burden of tourists.

Nor are children—despite the intimations of immortality Wordsworth claims for them—very conscious in their early childhood of either natural or supernatural beauty. It is a rare child who is alive to the bits and pieces and installments of a miracle such as spring. We kids growing up in the country did not notice the young willows down by the creek turning butter-yellow until they dotted the drab and darkled spring landscape like bonfires. Nor did we notice the birthing of a fern, uncurling like a liberated foetus. Or the fact that even weeds aborning are things of beauty, and that one of spring's first exhibits in her art gallery is skunk cabbage. So I cannot join the chorus of the pseudo-nature-mystics and child-romanticizers who promise that if children are taken back to the land they will automatically recover healthy instincts, harmonious feelings, and organic relationships. At least, there very likely will be no quick consanguinity with nature, no prompt cures, no instant restoration of vital equilibrium.

But this I do know and can attest to: for the child fortunate enough to be born and reared in the real country (not just a "rural setting"), there is a rooting in the dark that bears a fruit at dawn which lasts past afternoon. And by its roots this fruit is known.

There is a mystery here I cannot quite fathom. I do not seem to have experienced nature in my early childhood in the Henry Jamesian way, with "an immense sensibility, a kind of huge spider-web of the finest silken thread suspended in the chamber of consciousness and catching every air-borne particle in its tissue." I do not remember falling on my knees in transcendent wonder and ecstasy upon discovering a Jack uncoiling its canopied pulpit. But I do so now. At least my spirit bows the knee to this prelate of the forest temple.

Did George Eliot touch the clue to the mystery in *The Mill on the Floss* when she wrote:

> We could never have loved the earth so well if we had no childhood in it . . . our delight in the sunshine or the deep-bladed grass today might be no more than the faint perception of wearied souls, if it were not for the sunshine and the grass in the far-off years which still live in us, and transform our perception into love. There is no sense of ease like the ease we felt in those scenes where we were born, where objects became dear to us before we had known the labor of choice, and where the outer world seemed only an extension of our own personality: we accepted and loved it as we accepted our sense

of existence and our own limbs . . . . and there is no better reason for preferring this elderberry bush than that it stirs an early memory—that it is no novelty in my life, speaking to me merely through my present sensibilities to form and color, but the long companion of my existence, that wove itself into my joys when joys were vivid.

I, too, have an elderberry bush that stirs an early memory. My way-past-noon elderberry bush is on an old logging road through our woodlot south of town. When I visit its bold birthing early in the spring, I am visiting the clump of elderberry bushes along the stretch of creek that flowed out of the pasture and alongside the road, safe from trampling hooves of cows and horses. When I sample my daughter's wine-red elderberry jelly, I am sampling with all my senses the dark heavy fruit that hung on a youngberry tree. For it is no novelty to my life, "speaking to me merely through my present sensibilities . . ."

Is this why I delight more in finding dog-tooth-violets, spring beauties, bloodroots, Dutchman's-breeches, wild phlox, trilium, marsh marigolds, and jack-in-the-pulpits in our Minnesota woods than I delight in finding yellow ladyslippers in our southern Minnesota woods and bunchberry flowers in our northern woods? There were no showy yellowslippers or white-petalled bunchberry flowers in my Taylor County woods—at least they did not show themselves to me. But the other wild flowers were there, and if they did not forcibly impress my external eye, they imprinted themselves on my inward eye so vividly that my present joy in them has the combined vividness of that ambiguous past and palpable present joy.

> Earth's crammed with heaven,
> And every common bush afire with God,
> But only he who sees takes off his shoes—
> The rest sit round it and pluck blueberries

wrote Elizabeth Barrett Browning. Just when did I take off my shoes to nature—that is, recognize its gifts and be moved to a conscious love for it? I am not sure. I suspect that it was about the same time I recognized the gifts I had received and continue to receive at the hands of God and was moved to love him—consciously. Which came first—nature or grace? Did I feel gratitude first for nature, his work? Or for grace, his gift? Or were the two loves aroused in me simultaneously, and they built upon each other?

Most of this "building up" of the two loves in a child is done, I suspect, by imperceptible daily deposits as thin as gossamer. Neither the child nor the child-watchers are aware of anything happening. But for some children there are "engulfing moments," as Wallace Stevens calls them—those fleeting fractions of time when the plugs and stops to the inner being are pulled for one brief infusion of glory. Magnificat moments. At such times the child's senses tell him to "take off his shoes," and he does. The moment is swiftly gone, but the child is never the same child.

One such time for me was the first time I con-

sciously saw and heard winter capitulate, saw with amazement the sun-stabbed snowdrifts, heard the invisible water slipping away under the belly of the snowbanks. I was behind the woodshed, and it could have been early April. The world was still winter-silent. No birds sang. But suddenly that liberating sound of snow water—eddies and streamlets forming in the dark cave of winter, the tide of spring alive and faintly stirring there below me. I sat on the chopping block, hugging my knees and listening, stretching and growing in every fiber of my inner being. Mother's shrill call shattered my engulfing moment, and I joined my family at the supper table. No one seemed to notice that my inner being had grown an inch. Or that I was on the way to becoming a lover. If they had noticed, if they had asked me with whom or with what I was falling in love, I could not have told them. Not then.

Lovers! Ultimately, it will not be the protect-our-environment, save-our-skin people who will save Mother Earth. It will be lovers, men and women and children who live in a life-giving, joy-giving relation-ship to nature because they live in a close and personal relationship to its creator. In the absence of this rela-tionship men cease to be lovers. Their daily lives shrink to a deaf-muted, eye-blinded, touch-taste-and-smell-blunted grotesqueness which no more resembles life than a raisin resembles a grape. Raisins, after all, are grapes divorced from the vines and roots!

But lovers are lovers because they have a sense of wonder! And if there is no sense of wonder? "If you could understand a single grain of wheat you would die of wonder," said the good Dr. Martin Luther. "The trouble with Erasmus is that he is not stupified with wonder at the child in the womb. He does not praise and thank God for the marvel of a flower or the bursting of a peach stone by the swelling seed. He beholds these wonders like a cow staring at a new gate."

Luther, Luther, if you had written like that in your catechism, a Taylor County farm girl would not have drubbed the sheepshed roof with the scuffed toes of her shoes as she lay there trying to memorize "body and soul, eyes, ears and all my members" and "clothing and shoes, meat and drink, house and home, wife and child, land, cattle and all my goods . . . for all of which I am in duty bound to thank and praise, to serve and obey him."

Aha, has Luther been sabotaged? Have Protestant children been fed just the barley soup of "in duty bound to thank and praise, serve and obey him" and been denied the sweet grapes of wonder that are plentifully to be picked in Luther? Is this one of the reasons why so many children who go through the graded curriculum of Sunday school and confirmation do not carry through into maturity the great gift of a natural sense of wonder? And why do so many of the "graduates" of the system drop out of church? For worship is transcendent wonder, and if the *natural* sense of wonder, which is God's creation, his *work*, is eroded, then God's grace, *his gift*, may more readily be ignored or refused. No grace, no gratitude! "Gratitude? To whom? For what?" asks the blessing-blind dropout. "Everything I've got I earned myself. I've got it coming." "Nothing is due me, everything is a gift!" says anyone with a lively sense of blessing.

Thanks be to God, what Alice Meynell called "the two high childhoods in the heart of man"—the love of nature and the love of the divine—grew apace in me. Yet I must have been troubled in my teens by the thought that the church was not properly tending and cultivating the humble grain of wonder sown by God in the ground of each child-soul. When I was forty, I found a poem I wrote in my teens and had since forgotten.

> I take my thoughts to church
> with prayer books in their hands.
> They fling them through the stained windows
> and dance gleefully up the slivers of sun.
> Impious children!
> *O, take me with!*
>
> My thoughts peel off their stocking
> and turn handsprings in the grass.
> A bird in the deep woods calls.
> My thoughts scamper away with bare feet.
> Unholy ones!
> *Oh, joy blessed!*
>
> Willow buds bursting—
> tinkles of laughter in the April breeze.
> Little hands smooth away withered leaves.
> Soft lips kiss green buds in the watery mould.
> Oh, you wild ones!
> *Ah, my beloveds!*

I entitled it (when I was forty!) "The Metaphysical Schism." Praise the Lord, it had been only a hair-line crack in my being and had left no scar. None whatsoever.

The Love of Creatures 7

As a rule, child sensibilities are not keenly attentive to many of the minutiae of nature, and we Hatlestad kids did not break the rule. But sometimes nature in Taylor County sent us a flood of impressions, and our senses simply had to come to their senses. For example, they simply could not and did not miss the aural impact of the full frog orchestra that suddenly began playing late in April. The spring peepers! Those incredible tiny creatures just awakened from winter sleep that play their liquid flutes in the ditches and sloughs and swamps and raise a delirious and ecstatic litany to resurrection. Some of us who have heard nightingales at midnight in a foreign wood have not been more moved than we were and are by that invisible frog orchestra that plays for so short a time in the country in the spring. How fortunate we were to have been children in the 1920s before the swamps and sloughs were ditched and drained and dispossessed of spring peepers. The Day of the Peepers—Joseph Wood Krutch called it a moveable feast like Easter—has practically disappeared from the liturgical calendar of most children of the 70s.

If flutes and pipes and flageolets dominated the spring peeper orchestra, cellos and bass viols dominated the prairie chicken symphony that played at sundown in late April. We were ignorant in those days of the intricate ballet of courtship that accompanied this distant, dusky music. We knew for a certainty that we were listening to something that was mysterious and elemental and stirred some as-yet unplucked chords in our being. Later when in our meadow-scampering we surprised a frightened fluff of chicks, our minds made no connection whatsoever between them and the symphony concert we had heard. We did not realize at the time that we were listening to "Overture to the Prairie Chicks."

As a matter of fact, we kids of the 20s were kept so innocent of sex that we practically never associated kittens with cat-copulations or lambing or calving with ramming and rutting. All babies—be they human, beast, or fowl—were pure gift, and spring was Christmas all over again with rapturous gifts of kittens, puppies, lambs, piglets, calves, and foals. They came with all the surprise of Christmas gifts. We discovered them with an ecstasy of delight when we visited the barn these days and promptly dropped on our knees to adore these barn babies, still wet behind their ears. We learned the grief of loss from these gifts, too, for not infrequently we discovered in a barn visit the cold stiff body of a kitten that had decided to sleep in the straw under the spreading canopy of a cow's stomach and never woke up again, for the cow also had decided to take a nap. We mourned for them without shame and buried them under crude crosses in our Pet Cemetery with dignity and ceremony. Blessed are their memories!

Imperceptible layers of enrichment were also mysteriously deposited in our inner beings on summer evenings when we took the cows down a seldom-travelled road to the night pasture a quarter of a mile away. The cows, relieved of udder pressure, ambled in a state of animal bliss. Their winter of joyless, juiceless hay was past, and the future of summer heat and maddening flies had not yet come. Kids and cows took their time, for time was now, and now was a pleasure. The walk home again was even slower, for arrival home meant going to bed. If it became so dark that we stepped accidentally into cow-pies, it really did not matter, for mother was one who made us wash our feet every night no matter what. We envied the Schmidt kids whose mother did not.

It was then that we absorbed the night sounds and night sights so deeply that they have never slipped away. The stars came out, the moon waxed or waned, the frogs croaked. And the whippoorwill sang! By day kids are so flooded by sense impressions that they do not as a rule heed the songs of birds. Daytime is a symphony in which one does not hear the single flute or cello or violin. But nighttime is not even a chamber orchestra. In the theater of our June nights the whippoorwill came onstage and sang an unaccompanied solo—sang with such passion that even our kid callousness or complacency was stirred with a feeling of cosmic loneliness and longing. But not for long! Before we reached home, the fireflies had turned on. After all, we were only kids, so we shook off the intimations of infinity for the finite fun of catching and cupping in our hands that cold flame that still is an enigma to man. Moonflame he can explain, but not firefly flame!

Like so much else, awareness of nature is caught, not taught. Attempts to teach it to us seemed always to fail. For example, The First-Bird Contest, which was invented, I am sure, "to build awareness of nature." Each and every new teacher we had—and they changed almost every year—optimistically attempted the First Bird Contest. About mid-March we arrived at school and found a neat chart decorated with pictures of birds on the bulletin board. There were three columns: *Name of Bird Seen—Name of Child Who Saw Bird—Date Seen*. The chart never survived longer than two weeks. Inevitably in its second week it was taken down without any explanation or apology. After all, grownups do not as a rule explain or apologize for their flops and failures.

We older kids needed no explanation. We knew why the First Bird game could never be played in a room full of imaginations so fertile and extravagant that they often could not distinguish between fact and fiction. The younger the pupil, the more nebulous the space between the two. We older kids reported our sightings honestly, cross-our-hearts-hope-to-die. But hands shot up all over the room and shot down our testimony. If Jim Weber reported seeing a robin March 25, Lily Sorenson had seen one the week previous, but seven-year-old Angeline Smeby had seen one on Valentine's Day!

The robins returned in April unheralded and uncharted!

But it was not the ecumenical world of flocks and herds, of birds and beasts, that invested my ground as much as it was individual created beings. Much is being said and written about the mystery of imprinting in the world of living things. Various experiments with ducklings, fledgling pheasants, and grouse, are demonstrating that humans, too, can imprint their human images on feathered creatures. But imprinting may be a double process. The life of a human does indeed subtly touch the life of a creature, but the life of a creature also subtly touches the life of a human. Creatures that receive tender human love change themselves into us, but we who receive tender creaturely love change ourselves into them as well. Always and always it is a one-to-one relationship—one particular human and one particular creature in one particular place at one particular time. And one particular trusting intimate relationship established in the newfledged years of two who share the same Creator is the door to all future trusting intimate human-creature relationships.

Just as in inter-human relationships there is a "too-late! too late!" so also in human-creature relation-

ships. The unloved human infant grows into an adult unable to relate in love to anybody. A child who has never had one trusting intimate relationship to any creature grows into an adult who is either indifferent to creatures or finds it painful and difficult to relate to them.

How grateful I am that I was crony to particular horses, particular cows, particular dogs, particular cats! Personal relationships they were, every one of them. We were kith and kin, the creatures and I, for we belonged to each other. We were in relationship. Each one of them helped keep out of threat and out of bounds the impersonal anonymous world that is man's creation, the world that has grown to such vast proportions that it threatens to engulf the world of the personal, the world of relationships. Does a tractor lift its head when it hears your approaching step and shrilly neigh a welcome—or stretch its head and nuzzle and nibble your sleeve and collar? Does a motorcycle rush to meet you with wagging tail and bark and beam its preposterous devotion? Does a vacuum cleaner leap to your lap and, stroking some internal harp, play a thrumming song?

Home for us eight was a nest of warm human love. I thank my Creator that my humans permitted it to be a place of creature love. To come home from school to accepting parents was a blessing which I understand and am fully aware of only now. It was a given I took for granted at the time. To come home from school and be lunged at by a rushing streak of black and licked by a lolling tongue was a joy I fully understood then and there. How could one possibly take it for granted? How could one possibly be indifferent to such a tempest of affection? Or grow up indifferent?

There is a parabolic truth in Hans Christian Andersen's charming story "The Emperor and the Nightingale." The surface truth is that the Emperor was happy and healthy as long as his relationship to the nightingale was personal and childlike, full of humility and free of egotism. Not "This creature is mine, my possession. It exists for my personal satisfaction." But "This nightingale comes to me. Incredible, for I do not deserve it! Nevertheless, it comes to me and sings to me, and its singing gives me the deepest joy!"

When the Emperor became insensitive to the real nightingale and appropriated and possessed in selfishness and pride the impersonal mechanical copy of the nightingale, his life wasted away and almost died. The real nightingale returned to him—or, more correctly, he returned to the personal relationship with the real bird just in time.

The parabolic truth of the story is that the relationship between man and nature which witnesses to Creator is life-giving, joy-giving. A relationship between man and an impersonal, mechanical world that only witnesses to absence slowly emaciates and mutilates the life of the spirit.

It was in Hans Christian Andersen's native country that I learned this lesson all over again. It is never easy for children to enter school in a foreign country, but nine-year-old Theodore's enrollment in a small rural school in southern Sjaelland was eased by the venerable teacher's beautiful collie. Invited into the schoolroom on my son's miserable first day (I suspect to make what happened happen), the collie thrust his nose on Theodore's knee and gazed at him with limpid, soulful eyes. Misery vanished, and shy boy enrolled in the kingdom of dogdom as well as a foreign school that had frightened him—but no more.

"We went for a walk in the big woods across the Susaa bridge today," he announced upon coming home some days later. "We were gone all morning."

"Oh? That must have been interesting. I suppose Herr Nielsen taught you the names of trees and plants and stones and things?" I prompted, at once curious about the possible pedagogical justification for such an extended escape from the school room.

"Naw! He just let us walk and run and have fun! We took Bamse along. He has to be on a leash in the woods because there are pheasants and roe deer. We saw some pheasants. They whooshed up right under our noses."

Apparently caressing the smooth orange-gold head of a dog was no random movement. There seemed to be a mysterious connection between loving a soulful-eyed collie and learning the multiplication tables. Did Theodore's gentle old teacher know this? Had he had special training in Integrating Techniques? Was he representative of a new system of Total Teaching?

Theodore's father snorted when I voiced these thoughts to him.

"If Herr Nielsen had a doctor's degree in Gladsome Guidance and Jolly Counselling, if he were teaching by a 'Keep-the-pupils-happy' rule of thumb and motivating through mirth, then he would be turning out for the most part silly, presumptuous, and insolent pupils. No, Herr Nielsen is a wonderful oddity in this age—an unfragmented man. He knows what it is to be a total man, a whole man. If he represents anything, it is humanity—deep, sound humanity—common sense so fundamental that it is uncommon, simplicity so unaffected that it is profound, and joy so natural that it is supernatural."

Bamse, the golden collie, was instantly killed one March day by a speeding car. The school children were unconsolable. Herr Nielsen's tears were quiet but unashamed. The burial in a corner of the flower garden was reverent and dignified.

Theodore asked the inevitable question "Is Bamse in heaven?"

"There was a great Spanish poet, Unamuno, who wrote a poem to his dog when it died. He thinks the spirit of things we love on earth will be in heaven—even the spirit of trees, the spirit of rivers."

Theodore lifted a shining face. "Let's send the poem to Herr Nielsen when we get home!"

We did.

When Tivoli opened May 1, the great discovery for Theodore was not the flea circus or the boat rides on the miniature lake or the fabulous fireworks, but the machine which for twenty-five øre pressed out letters on a shine piece of metal. After three tries and as many misspelled, misspaced failures, Theodore finally succeeded in getting a good impression of—not his own name and address—but

BAMSE NIELSEN, NAESBY SKOL, DIED 1960

"It's for Herr Nielsen to fix on a nice piece of wood and put up on Bamse's grave," he exclaimed.

The Gospel of Silence

8

*The terrestrial ball of my childhood was not a noise-*crazed planet, an orbiting acoustic inferno. Silence had not as yet been banished from the earth and exiled to outer space. Compared to the traffic-roaring roads of today, the highways and lowways of the earth of my childhood were ribbons of silence. The quietness of lakes was not shattered by loud-mouthed motorboats. Snowmobiles, screaming at the top of their lungs, did not hunt down and kill white winter stillness. Radio, TV, hi-fi, and Muzak had not moved in, rudely occupied the space that belongs to silence, and proceeded to cheapen and make incessant demands upon our sensibilities. Thus I was able in my childhood to accumulate silence and fill the reservoir

of my inner being with it. That supply of natural silence seems to be limitless, enabling me to draw on it and be refreshed in today's world, where silence is a forsaken, forgotten grace and noise has become *natural*.

Even when I was a child, my being seemed to crave times of silence and solitude, for I was always consciously or unconsciously selecting the errands, chores, and assignments that provided such times. Plucking mustard in the field of young corn, picking potato bugs, hoeing the garden were not always jobs that fell to my lot. As a rule they were options that I chose, preferring these tasks only because I could do them alone. Fetching the cows from a distant pasture was fun in concert with Eleanor and Bernard, but when I did it solo, it was an inpouring into that secret reservoir of silence. The cows, those great hulks of silence, had nothing to say as they slouched along to night pasture. (A Yiddish proverb declares: if the horse had anything to say, he would speak up.)

More often than not I closed the gate on them and went on walking around the section. Two of the four miles were uninhabited—the other two but sparsely. I walked into sunsets that sometimes turned the clouds into flaming towers of silence. I walked past the sunsets into dusks that blessed me with their silence. I can think of no other reason for those solitary walks than that I felt blessed. It was well-meaning but distinctly infelicitous of Margaret, on vacation from work in the big, bad city of Chicago, to inquire where I was one July evening and, upon hearing that I was walking around the section unaccompanied, filled my parents with stories of kidnappings, rapes, and murders of guileless girls. My walks alone at dusk were abruptly halted.

But there were plenty of islands of silence in my Taylor County kingdom, and I did not mourn too long the vanishing of one of them.

What actually happened in those frequent intervals of solitude and silence that blessed my childhood?

Some daydreaming, of course, for what girl does not dream of the prince that will come—some day! But Hollywood and movie magazines were not yet feeding rural maidens silly, romantic, impossible dreams. My prince was not a movie actor but a forest ranger, and we were going to live in a virgin forest far away and be intimate with deer and all the creatures of the wood. In fact, my imagination flirted with the birds and animals more than with my prince, and the first stories I began writing secretly at the age of nine were about them, not him.

But what was answered in my never-never-lonely aloneness was not a craving for a perfect mate but the deep craving of the deeper self for man's lost home. The answer to that craving did not come in voices, flashes, and other private revelations but in faint squibs of perception that could hardly be called meanings but certainly were a becoming. Not in thoughts and conclusions shaped at the center of the mind, but in a widening and enlarging of the attentiveness and receptivity at the center of the soul.

When the Greek god Amor left the mortal maid Psyche after a secret night visit, he said, "You will give birth to a divine child if you keep silent, a mere human if you betray the secret." Commenting on that myth, Kierkegaard said: "Every human being who knows how to keep silent becomes a divine child, for in silence there is concentration upon his divine origin; he who speaks remains a human being."

But to be human is to know one's divine origin. A human who never comes to that knowledge is never truly human. The calamity of our noisy secularized age is that the hints and clues that lead to that discovery are so few, so few! And the few that there are cannot be heard for the clamor. Man has bulldozed a great gulf of noise between himself and the eternal, paradoxically creating for himself a silence and isolation that screams of absence. For there is a bad silence as well as a good silence and solitude. Under any good silence and solitude there is a better silence and solitude where Spirit whispers to spirit: "Your origin is no secret! The Eternal and Infinite God is truly your Father, Abba." Under any bad silence and solitude there is a worse silence and solitude that thunders in decibels of noise: "You ask your origin? Blind fate and blind force washed you up on the beach of time. You are an accident that took on flesh and bone. You are a metaphysical bastard."

The harm that the modern media have done to addict children to noise, to take noise for granted—indeed, not to dare be alone and surrounded by silence—is incalculable! The things of nature are filled with silence. The things man invents are loud and loquacious. For the most part animals maintain a monastic silence. Man has created media with a mania for saying something when there is nothing to say. To this travesty of words and other sounds man has learned to listen without listening. He asks no questions and gets no answers. Indeed, he expects no answers. The modern child exposed night and day to boxes that emit sounds develops a mania for listening to sounds that communicate meaninglessness. The problem—and it is a crisis problem—is how to teach children to dial silence and not a TV channel, to reach for silence instead of a top-ten record.

Approximately one hundred and fifty years ago Kierkegaard wrote in *For Self-Examination:* "When one considers the present state of the world and the whole of life, he is obliged Christianly to say (Christianly he is certainly justified in saying it!): 'What do you think must be done?' I would answer: 'The first thing, the unconditional condition on which anything can be done, is: Silence! Bring about silence! God's Word cannot be heard. If, served by noisy mediators, it has to be shouted clamorously in order to be heard in the hubbub and racket, it does not remain God's Word. Bring about silence! Everything is noise! . . . And man, sharp wit that he is, does not sleep in order that he may invent new, ever new means of increasing noise, of circulating uproar and triviality with the greatest possible haste and on the greatest possible scale. Everything is soon turned upside down. As far as significance is concerned, communication has soon reached its lowest point, and at the same time as far as speedy and overflowing propagation is concerned, communicators have just about reached their highest point. For what is got out in such hot haste, and—on the other hand, what has a greater circulation than—gossip! Bring about silence! ' "

Is it any wonder that when my partner and I translated those words in 1940 my Taylor County lake of silence nudged the shores of my consciousness and registered a quiet ripple of approval?

Anyone who writes a gospel of silence must in all honesty admit that silence may be demonic instead of divine. Simply not to be talking is not the same as silence: it may be silent despair, hopelessness. To be alone is not the same as solitude: it may be a terrible alienation. A desire for solitude does not always mean that there is still a measure of spirit in a person. It may mean that spirit is exercising no power over a person's life, that he is defeated and fearful. He may have shut himself away from society, shut himself up with his private demons.

Whether the "old bachelors" who lived in somewhat more than a normal quota in our township were victims of a demonic silence I was too young and inexperienced to know. Their hermit life in tar-paper shacks piqued our curiosity. What did they eat? Did they ever take a bath? Did they have any relatives anywhere on earth? Were they escaped convicts? Had they run away from nagging wives?

Mother refused to let our old bachelor neighbors isolate themselves totally. Every once in a while she sent father to invite one of them to what she called "a square meal." That is, a meal that measured up qualitatively and quantitatively to a good farmwife's rule of thumb. That is, a meal of meat, potatoes, gravy, vegetables, homebaked bread, homemade butter, and apple pie. If the invited bachelor had a private demon, it was temporarily defeated by the memory of other meals at our house. Moreover, the demon was left behind in the tar-paper shack, and the bachelor came alone, as quietly courteous as any guest that graced our table.

We kids respected our guests' secrets, both present and past, but that did not prevent us from playing private detectives and pooling our clues and conjectures later, fabricating fantastic biographies for them. One of the bachelors we decided was the disinherited son of a multimillionaire. After all, he knew how to use a knife and fork properly—even to laying the knife across the edge of the plate after using it and not placing it on the tablecloth to leave an ugly grease stain. We had learned this ourselves from mother, who in turn had learned it working as a maid in a rich man's family in southern Minnesota. Another one of our taciturn guests we decided had been a member of a Chicago gang but had repented his life of crime, and to save himself from being gunned down in the street by the mob had fled to northern Wisconsin. Our clues were impressive: a downcast look, a nervous tic, and a certain jumpiness when a strange car drove into the yard. Only when he learned that it was the Watkins peddler on his twice-a-year visit with soaps and lotions and spices and vanilla did he consent to a second piece of pie. Even so he left very quickly after the noon meal, forgetting to take the loaf of bread and sack of oatmeal cookies mother had told him she had set out for him on the kitchen chair where he had hung his jacket.

It was mother who once in a blue moon manifested another kind of demonic silence—the proud, cold, silent treatment. It was always father who was the victim. We children never knew the whys and wherefores. A hint of beer on father's breath when he returned from town? Buying something he really did not need at an auction? Whatever the reason, mother occasionally clammed up and for some days refused to communicate with father. The climate of house and home suddenly turned arctic. Meals were eaten in silence. Father tried lamely to communicate with us children, but our words died before they were born. Mother's silence was too visible and too violent. It beat upon us more harshly than the blows of sound.

A dozen years later I worked with a girl whose parents had not spoken to each other for fifteen years. That demonic silence showed tragically in their daughter. She could not cope. Every new job, every new situation, every new relationship was a threat she could not meet. Fortunately mother's private demon was soon sent packing and father was returned to her good graces. But my sisters and I vowed early that we would never use silence as a weapon in our families. Better by far to blister the husband in a passionate torrent of hot words than freeze him in a silence more deadly than the silence of the grave!

We children were saved from damage, I am positive, because 98% of the time the silences between mother and father were summery silences, not wintry ones. For example, summer evenings on the front porch after the chores were done, mother and father swung comfortably, tranquilly, and quietly in the porch swing while we kids caught and cupped fire-flies. Or, as bedtime drew near, we sat on the porch steps keeping our bodies and tongues in stillness lest we remind the parents of our presence and be sent to bed. We listened and heard the things mother and father refrained from saying, and that unspoken conversation was so amiable and cozy that we felt like yearling calves in clover.

Much much later I recognized that same silence which is infinitely good to listen to in the white spaces in poetry. The things an excellent poem refrains from saying are delightful, exquisite!

Not one of the Hatlestad clan grew up to be what mother called a windbag, but only one of us adopted silence as a native tongue. Joseph was, is, and remains a man of few words. His speech and his flashes of quick wit—when they come—come out of the full-ness of his long silences. Earth turns quietly for him. To be in the presence of this quiet brother is to have the screeching gyration of one's own spinning planet lubricated with the oil of silence. Sharing his silence is not disquieting—in fact, it is like rain solitude when the gray sky drops down and space shrinks to a cell, a sanctuary. Sharing his silence is to share his modest and humble sense of the modest and humble gifts of God. That he never lost this sense is due in some part, I am sure, to the simple kind of farming he has been doing for half a century in Taylor County, Wisconsin.

No Ground Too Fallow

9

If my radical student friend is still reading this, still hoping for that knot to be tied, he no doubt is fit to be tied himself. I can just hear him saying it: "Your pious-sounding gratefulness for what you seem to consider your superlatively great past is nothing but smug self-complacency. Your eulogizing your past is just a sugar-coating of your personal prejudices and rigid formalism and bigoted moralism. I suspect that you see yourself—if I may be permitted to juggle history a bit—as Molly Pitcher holding the Christian fort against the barbarian hordes."

"Maybe so! Maybe so!" I would say. "Self-deception is just as easy for me as for thee. May I just warn you of the smug self-complacency and rigid formal-

ism and bigoted moralism of your own pious relevances and bright, bright future—after you have
completely liberated yourselves, of course, from the
bad messy past we made for you."

And if my radical student friend and I could and
would throw away our respective generation's favorite clubs, maybe we could and would tie that knot
after all.

But what is the knot? And how can anyone know
when that knot is tied? The knot is the past, present,
and future tied together in a healthy and healthgiving relationship. The knot is tied when someone
is able to affirm confidently and positively:

> I was.
> I am.
> I will be.
> I am because I was.
> I will be because I am.

Not until then is there a firm and healthy and unslippable knot. Until then there are only loose threads
and twisted strands and lint from the past cluttering
up the present.

Even a four-year-old can be as baffled by this knot
as by learning to tie her shoelaces. When Sara was
four, she pondered a picture postcard from Grandpa,
visiting the ancestral farm in Valdres, Norway, and
spoke a poem. Sara loves an aunt named Ann and
therefore calls ancestors "ann-sisters."

> I wish I lived in the olden times
> and could see my ann-sisters.

116

I wish I could see them—
and stay young.
But that's a problem!
I can't live *before.*

Sara, I predict, will really have no problem living
before and after at the same time in any present, for
the ground in which her being is growing is as good,
if not better, than mine ever was. It is they who feel
that they had a real or imagined bad past who have
real or imagined problems tying a firm, healthy, unslippable knot, of living in a healthy relationship to
the past, present, and future.

But what if the ground of the past really was no
good, no ground at all? Perhaps the cracked concrete
of a ghetto jungle? Perhaps the trash-filled scrabble
of an old garbage dump, reeking of rancid hatreds
and stale animosities? And what if the ground of the
present is no better?

There are gloomsters who say that the easy tilth of
the past in which the human plant gathered its soil-
food and soulfood can never be recovered again. The
current craze for the nostalgic, they say, is not a last
tango on the shores of memory but people ship-
wrecked in the present frantically grabbing for float-
ing planks. Having demolished the ships called Institution, Tradition, Establishment (in fact, made those
many-lettered words into dirty words), having re-
duced man to simply man himself, we find ourselves
in the nightmarish situation of being unable to provide for our own and our children's deepest needs and
of not knowing where to turn for help. Our turning

to the past is but the desperate admission that we have broken under the strain of the present and cannot face the future. In other words, prognosticators in today's world see no happy ending to our present predicament. "We are ruined!" they cry.

To which the radical young would cry, "Ruined, yes! But the ruin is all your making—you the Establishment have fouled the planet and set it on a disaster course." And the generations begin swinging their favorite clubs at each other all over again.

Bad pasts—so there are. But when were there not? Creatures of crisis—so we are. But when were we not? And where in the Word does it say that we are totally abandoned to poor ground, to bad pasts, and a crisis present—if so they really be? Only in modern literature are stupidity and depravity the last word about man. I much prefer the words of an ancient poet named Hosea:

Break up the fallow ground,
for there is yet time to seek the Lord.

Deluges come and deluges go, crises come and crises go, and the Captain Noahs of the Unsinkable Good Ship Faith send out the dove, and the bird comes back, in the life of faith it always comes back, and always bearing the sticky green leaf of hope. Always the same dove bearing the same olive leaf—the hope, the promise, that his Holy Spirit can and will break up the hardpan soil for the roots of being! He, the Divine Plowman, can and will do it. And whether or not the soil is old, pooped out, washed out, worn out—or no soil at all. Whether or not the time is so long, so dreadfully long. Or short, so short! "For there is yet time . . ." As long as time is there, there is time to be cultivated by the Divine Plowman and salvaged by the Divine Salvager.

We are said to be living in a climate of unfaith, to be entering the post-Christian era. But the worse the weather, someone has said, the better the weather is—for faith! May not his Holy Oddity be immersing our hallowed but perhaps hollowed traditions and institutions and establishments in the consuming and purifying fire of his Spirit so that they may be renewed? May he not be rinsing our culture clean of Christianity so that once again it is manifestly clear what it truly means to be a Christian? May he not be making Christianity once again "that scandalous thing" it was in the beginning? Is it possible for us who are so accustomed to having him come at us in credible straightforward and conventional ways to understand that it is possible for him to come incredibly and askew?

"If I catch sight of an invincible, insubmersible, incomprehensible Christianity creeping out again from below, creeping in from the surroundings, creeping in from all around," wrote the French poet Peguy at the beginning of this century, "am I to miss my chance of hailing it just because I was not up to calculating where it would come from? . . . Where is it written that God will abandon man to sin? . . . This people will finish a way they never began, this age, this world, this people will get there along a road they never set out on."

But sure as I am that God's Divine Plowman can cultivate any ground or unground, I am just as sure that the gift of God which is called grace cannot develop without that work of God which is called nature. Sure as I am that it is grace which takes the initiative and the heart responds, I am just as sure that the heart has a harder time of it when it has no tilth and when its natural disposition is to dread or to refuse every spiritual gift.

Therefore I pray a paradoxical prayer. I ask him who plows my soul's soil to refine out of it whatever was or is or has become false. In the same breath I thank him for the minimum of natural substance that is capable of bearing fruit. And that it may under his cultivation bear fruit into my oldest age, that even my point-of-death fruit may not be crabbed and sour. If I could not pray that prayer, I would be unable to remember my past with joy and gratitude, unable to live in every present and without fear of the future.

Is it smug self-complacency, self-satisfied pietism, blindness to the human condition—as my radical student friend thinks—for me to feel: "My upgrowing was good. My family was good. My church was good. My community, my friends were good." Is this a Pollyanna attitude, and does it affirm only what is compatible in life and reject what is incompatible? Is it not refusing to face one's own and life's existential absurdity?

Hardly! I would rather call it Christian realism, which admits to the presence of dark forces in the past, present, and future, accepts the inevitable ever-

lasting struggle with these dark forces in time in the name of Jesus Christ and is delivered from their power by the victory of Jesus Christ. Not delivered from the struggle, but set free from the past by gratitude to the past to engage in that everlasting struggle with cheerful confident courage.

Yes, set free by gratitude! He who knows he has been given can give. He who knows he has received can receive. He who has experienced faithfulness in his past knows how to be faithful. He who has learned that others can be relied on is inwardly motivated to be reliable. He who recognizes the good in his past can move confidently through a bad present into an uncertain future.

And even if there is not much to be grateful for, there is always something infinite for which one can be infinitely grateful—the forgiven past! The formula for grace is not as simple (or simplistic) as "I'm OK You're OK." It is: "Forgive me, as I forgive you, in the name and power of Jesus Christ, who forgives both you and me."

Thanks to this formula, I do not need to pay costly and weekly visits to a psychiatrist to be liberated from my own parents or my own past—that is, liberated from their "bad" qualities or the "badness" in my past. They were not gods who condemned me to worship them to my grave or live in a prison of guilt. They were not demons whom my own demons compel me to blame and resent all my born days. They and I were mortal beings with human natures, but we were not slaves to our human natures. Our human natures, the work of God, were basically good, but when and where they faulted and failed there began a love which was not our own. In that love we forgave each other our major and minor sins against each other, even as God forgave us the enormity of our sins against him.

Thus I do not and cannot celebrate the past as a better time than the present. Or celebrate the Here and Now *as it is* (another modern heresy, a cousin of the heresy which does not know the difference between celebration and entertainment!). I celebrate instead the everlasting presence and action of God in my past and my ever-so-concrete present. I celebrate him who is my hope for the future. There is no evil too horrible or scene too mundane for his transcending presence and action. Were I to speak only of the evil or the mundane, I would be giving them a perpetuity and wider horror and mundaneness than they had in their concreteness. Were I to celebrate life as it is, I would be denying the liberating power of God in the Here and Now. Were I to exalt the past over the present, I would be calling the present a hopeless desolation and God a helpless Has-Been. Were I to express hopelessness about the future, I would be practically an atheist—or an atheist in practice.

There are some well-grounded fears that "saving the planet" and the whole-earth philosophy is just another man-made religion, but may it not also be God at his eternal task of teaching men how to love and seeking always and by every conceivable means to dispose the world so that his supernatural love can take root? May not his Divine Oddity be coming at us from the oddest of places, especially at those of us who continue to play the lord of ourselves and of the universe? He knows that if we are allowed to keep on, there soon will be no natural ground to receive the divine gift of grace. His methods may be startling, but he is only trying to re-educate us.

"And there is only just time," declares Gustave Thibon, a modern French Hosea. "There is only just time to re-educate this poor nature, deprived by some inhuman dance—not before the ark of the Lord, but before the mirror of Narcissus—of the use of its ontological joints. And this in the interest of the supernatural itself, for if grace *edifies* (what an ominous sign of death that this splendid word has become funny!), it is always nature that provides the foundations."

No, son, I never did leave Taylor County, Wisconsin. And I ask once again the rhetorical question I asked in the beginning: "Why should I?" There in Taylor County, Wisconsin, I learned the ABC of my being. Learned it so well, in fact, that the XYZ part of my life will no doubt come not as a catastrophe but as a consummation. Because of that good childhood I suspect that in my agehood I will be able to say as serenely as the aged John Adams said to a visitor, "I inhabit a weak, frail decayed tenement; battered by the winds and broken in upon by the storms, and, from all I can learn, the landlord does not intend to repair."

Not that I am purblind to the baldheaded, bareboned facts of old age! My eyes have seen them coming my way, and my mind can conceive them as already arrived. But so bitter a picture as the English poet Matthew Arnold conceived in 1867 my eyes have not yet seen nor my mind foreseen:

GROWING OLD

What is it to grow old?
Is it to lose the glory of the form,
The luster of the eye?
Is it for beauty to forego her wreath?
—Yes, but not this alone.

Is it to feel each limb
Grow stiffer, every function less exact,
Each nerve more loosely strung?

Yes, this, and more; but not,
Ah, 'tis not what in youth we dreamed 'twould
  be!
'Tis not to have our life
Mellowed and softened as with sunset-glow,
A golden day's decline.

'Tis not to see the world
As from a height, with rapt prophetic eyes,
And heart profoundly stirred;
And weep, and feel the fullness of the past,
The years that are no more.
It is to spend long days
And not once feel that we were ever young;
It is to add, immured
In the hot prison of the present, month
To month with weary pain.

It is to suffer this,
And feel but half, and feebly, what we feel.
Deep in our hidden heart
Festers the dull remembrance of a change,
But no emotion—none. . . . .

Having never been a romanticist, I can agree with
Matthew Arnold that old age is by no means a "sunset-glow, a golden day's decline," but I ultimately
reject his bitter picture of old age as a frozen future,
"quite the phantom of ourselves." I turn from
Arnold's ghostly image of old age once again to the
April hope of Hosea:

Break up the fallow ground
For there is yet time to seek the Lord.

Even for a person with a body so decrepit that one
foot is already in the grave there is still time to cultivate the ground. In fact, to prohibit that frozen
old age Matthew Arnold described, it is absolutely
necessary to cultivate and to be cultivated. "For there
is yet time!" No ground is too old. No ground too
fallow.